RICHARD WAGNER

WESENDONCK-LIEDER

for Soprano and Orchestra

Ernst Eulenburg Ltd

London · Mainz · Madrid · New York · Paris · Tokyo · Toronto · Zürich

RICHARD WAGNER

Wesendonck-Songs

As a result of Wagner's active involvement in the abortive Dresden revolution of 1849, in which he was closely associated with the nihilist Bakunin, he was forced to flee from there, first to Weimar and then (using a false passport) to Switzerland, where he was supportecd by friends. His fame was growing – *Lohengrin and Tannhäuser* were making considerable headway, he became busy as a conductor in Zurich (and visited London in that capacity), and he wrote a number of articles and pamphlets besides working on the early parts of the *Ring* – but a return to Saxony was impossible on account of the warrant still out for his arrest. In 1857 Otto Wesendonck, a rich silk merchant, bought an estate just outside Zurich and generously allowed Wagner to occupy a cottage in the grounds at a nominal rent. Wesendonck's pretty, artistic young wife Mathilde had for some time been under Wagner's spell: there are references to her in the sketch for *Die Walküre*, and to her he had dedicated a piano sonata in E flat and the second version of his *Faust* overture.

On 1 January 1855 Wagner had written to Liszt, 'Since I have never, in my whole life, tasted the true happiness of love I intend raising a monument to that most beautiful of dreams, in which this love shall, for once, be utterly fulfilled. I have in mind a plan for *Tristan and Isolde*. . . .' The *affaire* he was conducting with Mathilde undoubtedly played some part in the formation of this plan, though it is likely that she was his projection of the old story's erotic atmosphere rather than the inspiration for it. By August 1857, fanned by Mathilde's propinquity, he had become so obsessed with the subject that he put aside *Siegfried* (in which he was nearing the end of Act 2) in order to work on the *Tristan* poem. Each evening he would read to Mathilde what he had written, and under its heady influence she herself wrote five passionate poems, which he set for voice and piano during that winter while working on the first act of the opera.

Der Engel, composed on 30 November, stylistically still inhabits the largely diatonic world of *Rheingold;* but *Träume* (4-5 December) looks forward to Act 2 of *Tristan*, where its theme appears in Brangäne's solo as she keeps vigil on the watchtower; *Schmerzen* (17 December, though much revised later) also begins with the initial chord of Act 2. *Stehe still* (whose third verse is conspicuously Tristanesque) did not follow until 22 February the following year, after Wagner had visited Paris – partly for business reasons, partly in an attempt to check the relationship with Mathilde, over which his wife Minna was, not unnaturally, becoming increasingly incensed. ('I am at the end of a conflict', he wrote to Liszt, 'in which is involved everything that can be sacred to a man; I must come to a decision.') In the first week of April, Minna intercepted a note Wagner had written to Mathilde with a sketch of the prelude to *Tristan* (whose first act he had just sent to his publishers, Breitkopf & Härtel). In the wake of the pent-up emotional storm which then broke, Minna was sent away to recover and the Wesendonks, to avoid scandal, went off to Italy. *Im Treibhaus,* the last of the Wesendonk songs to be composed, was dated 1 May: although by that time Wagner was sketching Act 2 of *Tristan,* the song anticipates the start of Act 3, which was not begun until his return from Venice the following March, by which time he had, with characteristic egotism, extricated himself from an *affaire* which by then had served its purpose.

The orchestral version of *Träume,* with a solo violin taking the vocal line, had been written by Wagner for performance under Mathilde's window on her 29th birthday (23 December 1857) – foreshadowing the genesis of the *Siegfried Idyll* almost exactly thirteen years later. The other songs were orchestrated very much later by his disciple Felix Mottl. In the present edition Wagner's keyboard originals are shown below the orchestral score.

Lionel Salter, 1979

RICHARD WAGNER

Wesendonck-Lieder

Da sich Wagner aktiv an der fehlgeschlagenen Dresdner Revolution von 1849 beteiligt und enge Beziehungen mit dem Nihilisten Bakunin aufgenommen hatte, sah er sich gezwungen, aus Dresden zu fliehen, zunächst nach Weimar, und später (mit einem falschen Pass) in die Schweiz, wo er von Freunden unterstützt wurde. Sein Ruhm verbreitet sich – die Erfolge von *Lohengrin* und *Tannhäuser* mehrten sich beträchtlich, und seine Beschäftigung als Dirigent in Zürich nahm zu (in dieser Eigenschaft kam er auch nach London). Ausserdem schrieb er eine Reihe von Artikeln und Flugschriften und arbeitete an den ersten Teilen des *Rings* – doch eine Rückkehr nach Sachsen war unmöglich, weil der für ihn ausgeschriebene Haftbefehl noch gültig war. Otto Wesendonck, ein wohlhabender Seidenhändler, kaufte 1857 ein Gut unweit Zürich. Er erlaubte Wagner grosszügig in einem Häuschen auf seinem Besitz für eine geringfügige Miete zu wohnen. Wesendoncks junge und hübsche, künstlerisch veranlagte Frau Mathilde stand schon seit einiger Zeit unter Wagners Bann. In der Skizze für die *Walküre* berief er sich stellenweise auf sie, und er widmete ihr die Klaviersonate in Es-Dur, sowie die zweite Fassung seiner *Faust-Ouvertüre.*

Wagner schrieb am 1. Januar 1855 an Liszt: ‚Da ich nun aber doch im Leben nie das eigentliche Glück der Liebe genossen habe, so will ich diesem schönsten aller Träume noch ein Denkmal setzen, in dem vom Anfang bis zum Ende diese Liebe sich einmal so recht sättigen soll: ich habe im Kopf einen *Tristan und Isolde* entworfen . . . .' Das Verhältnis mit Mathilde spielte zweifellos eine gewisse Rolle in der Gestaltung dieses Plans, obgleich es wahrscheinlich ist, dass sie für ihn eher die erotische Atmosphäre der alten Sage verkörperte, als ihn damit zu inspirieren. Anfang August 1857 war er, angespornt durch Mathildes Nähe, schon so von dem Thema besessen, dass er seinen *Siegfried* (dessen zweiten Akt er fast vollendet hatte) beiseite legte, um sich der Arbeit am Gedicht des *Tristan* zu widmen. Jeden Abend las er Mathilde vor, was er geschrieben hatte, und beeinflusst von dem berauschenden Eindruck, schrieb sie selbst fünf leidenschaftliche Gedichte, die er während des gleichen Winters für Gesang und Klavier vertonte, wobei er gleichzeitig am ersten Akt der Oper arbeitete.

Das am 30. November komponierte Lied, *der Engel,* ist noch in der weitgehend diatonischen Welt des *Rheingolds* befangen. Aber *Träume* (4.-5. Dezember) deutet schon auf den zweiten Akt des *Tristan;* dort erscheint das Thema des Lieds in Brangänes Solo, während sie auf dem Wachtturm Ausschau hält. *Schmerzen* (17. Dezember, wenn auch später erheblich revidiert) beginnt ebenfalls mit dem ersten Akkord des zweiten

Akts. *Stehe still* (dessen dritter Vers deutliche Beziehungen zu *Tristan* hat) folgte erst am 22. Februar des nächsten Jahres, nachdem Wagner nach Paris gereist war – teils aus geschäftlichen Gründen, teils in der Absicht, die Beziehung zu Mathilde einzuschränken, über die seine Frau Minna sich verständlicherweise immer mehr empörte. Dazu schrieb er an Liszt, dass er am Ende eines Konflikts wäre, in dem alles was dem Menschen heilig sein könnte verwickelt sei, und dass er zu einem Entschluss kommen müsse. In der ersten Aprilwoche fing Minna einen für Mathilde bestimmten Zettel ab, auf dem Wagner das Vorspiel zu *Tristan* skizziert hatte (kurz nach der Absendung des ersten Akts dieser Oper an seinen Verleger Breitkopf & Härtel). Als Folge auf den bisher unterdrückten Sturm der Gefühle, der dann ausbrach, wurde Minna zur Erholung verschickt, während die Wesendonks, um einen Skandal zu verhüten, nach Italien fuhren. Das letzte der Wesendonk-Lieder, das Wagner komponierte, *Im Treibhaus*, ist 1. Mai datiert. Obwohl Wagner um diese Zeit mit den Skizzen zum zweiten Akt des *Tristan* beschäftigt war, nimmt dieses Lied den Anfang des dritten Akts voraus, der erst nach seiner Rückkehr aus Venedig im folgenden März begonnen wurde. Zu dieser Zeit hatte er sich schon von dem Verhältnis, das nun weinen Zweck erfüllt hatte, mit seiner typischen Selbstsucht befreit.

Wagner hatte *Träume* auch in einer Fassung für Orchester geschrieben, in der eine Solovioline den Gesang vertritt. Diese Fassung war für eine Aufführung unter Mathildes Fenster an ihrem 29. Geburtstag (23. Dezember 1857) bestimmt – womit die Entstehung des *Siegfried-Idylls*, das fast auf den Tag dreizehn Jahre später entstand, vorweg genommen wurde. Die anderen Lieder wurden sehr viel später von seinem Schüler Felix Mottl instrumentiert. In der vorliegenden Ausgabe steht Wagners ursprüngliche Klavierfassung unter der Orchesterpartitur.

Lionel Salter, 1979
Deutsche Übersetzung Stefan de Haan

Wesendonck-Lieder

DER ENGEL

In der Kindheit frühen Tagen
Hört' ich oft von Engeln sagen,
Die des Himmels hehre Wonne
Tauschen mit der Erdensonne,

Dass, wo bang ein Herz in Sorgen
Schmachtet vor der Welt verborgen,
Dass, wo still es will verbluten,
Und vergehn in Tränenfluten,

Dass, wo brünstig sein Gebet
Einzig um Erlösung fleht,
Da der Engel nieder schwebt,
Und es sanft gen Himmel hebt.

Ja, es stieg auch mir ein Engel nieder,
Und auf leuchtendem Gefieder
Führt er ferne jedem Schmerz,
Meinen Geist nun himmelwärts!

Wesendonck Songs

THE ANGEL

In early days of childhood
I oft heard tell of angels
who exchange the supreme bliss
of heaven for the light of Earth,

so that where a heart languishes, weighed down
with care, hidden from the world,
and where it would quietly bleed to death
and perish in floods of tears,

and where its prayer ardently
pleads only for salvation,
there the angel floats down
and gently bears it heavenward.

Yes, an angel came down to me too,
and on radiant pinions carries
my spirit, far from every care,
aloft to heaven!

STEHE STILL!

Sausendes, brausendes Rad der Zeit,
Messer du der Ewigkeit;
Leuchtende Sphären im weiten All,
Die ihr umringt den Weltenball;
Urewige Schöpfung, halte doch ein,
Genung des Werdens, lass mich sein!

Halte an dich, zeugende Kraft,
Urgedanke, der ewig schafft!
Hemmet den Atem, stillet den Drang,
Schweiget nur eine Sekunde lang!
Schwellende Pulse, fesselt den Schlag;
Ende, des Wollens ew'ger Tag!

Dass in selig süssem Vergessen
Ich mög' alle Wonnen ermessen!
Wenn Aug' in Auge wonnig trinken,
Seele ganz in Seele versinken;
Wesen in Wesen sich wieder findet,
Und alles Hoffens Ende sich kündet;

Die Lippe verstummt in staunendem Schweigen,
Keinen Wunsch mehr will das Inn're zeugen:
Erkennt der Mensch des Ew'gen Spur,
Und löst dein Rätsel, heil'ge Natur!

BE STILL!

Rushing, rumbling wheel of Time,
you measure of eternity;
shining spheres in the wide universe,
you that circle the globe of Earth;
primeval Creation, call a halt;
enough of evolving; let me be!

Stay awhile, generative force,
primal thought that is ever at work!
Hold your breath, curb your impetus,
be silent for but a second's length!
Surging pulse, shackle your pounding;
have done, eternal day of Will,

so that in blissful, sweet oblivion
I may savour utter rapture!
When eye drinks rapture from eye,
soul is wholly engulfed in soul,
being finds itself again in being
and learns the fulfilment of every hope,

then lips are dumb in astonished silence,
the inmost self formulates no further wish:
Man perceives the trace of Eternity
and solves your riddle, holy Nature!

IM TREIBHAUS

Hoch gewölbte Blätterkronen,
Baldachine von Smaragd,
Kinder ihr aus fernen Zonen,
Saget mir warum ihr klagt?

Schweigend neiget ihr die Zweige,
Malet Zeichen in die Luft,
Und der Leiden stummer Zeuge,
Steiget aufwärts süsser Duft.

Weit in sehnendem Verlangen
Breitet ihr die Arme aus,
Und umschlinget wahnbefangen
Öde Leere nicht'gen Graus.

Wohl ich weiss es, arme Pflanze:
Ein Geschicke teilen wir,
Ob umstrahlt von Licht und Glanze,
Unsre Heimat ist nicht hier!

Und wie, froh die Sonne scheidet
Von des Tages leerem Schein,
Hüllet der, der wahrhaft leidet,
Sich in Schweigens Dunkel ein.

Stille wird's, ein säuselnd Weben
Füllet bang den dunklen Raum:
Schwere Tropfen seh' ich schweben
an der Blätter grünem Saum.

IN THE HOTHOUSE

High-arching crowns of leaves,
canopies of emerald,
you children from far-off climes,
tell me, why do you grieve?

Silently you bow your branches,
paint sketches in the air,
and your sweet fragrance rises up,
mute witness of sorrow.

In yearning longing
you stretch out wide your arms
and in delusion embrace the empty
horror of a desolate void.

Well I know it, poor plant:
we share one fate,
that though surrounded by light
and brightness, our home is not here!

And as the sun gladly departs
from the blank light of day,
so one who truly suffers
wraps himself in the dark of silence.

It grows quiet: a rustling tremor
fills the dark room with dread;
I see heavy teardrops hovering
on the leaves' green edges.

SCHMERZEN

Sonne, weinest jeden Abend
Dir die schönen Augen rot,
Wenn im Meeresspiegel badend
Dich erreicht der frühe Tod;

Doch ersteh'st in alter Pracht,
Glorie der düstren Welt,
Du am Morgen neu erwacht,
Wie ein stolzer Siegesheld!

Ach, wie sollte ich da klagen,
Wie, mein Herz, so schwer dich sehn,
Muss die Sonne selbst verzagen,
Muss die Sonne untergehn?

Und gebieret Tod nur Leben,
Geben Schmerzen Wonnem nur:
O wie dank' ich, dass gegeben
solche Schmerzen mir Natur!

SORROWS

Every evening, sun, you weep
till your lovely eyes are red,
when, bathing in the ocean's mirror,
an early death claims you.

Yet you rise in your former splendour,
glory of the gloomy world,
newly awakened in the morning,
like a proud conquering hero!

Ah, why then should I complain,
my heart, why look on you so sadly,
if the sun itself must despair,
if the sun must founder?

And if death brings forth life
and sorrows only bring delight,
O how thankful am I that Nature
granted me such sorrows!

TRÄUME

Sag?, welch wunderbare Träume
Halten meinen Sinn umfangen,
Dass sie nicht wie leere Schäume
Sind in ödes Nichts vergangen?

Träume, die in jeder Stunde,
Jedem Tage schöner blüh'n,
Und mit ihrer Himmelskunde
Selig durch's Gemüte ziehn?

Träume, die wie hehre Strahlen
In die Seele sich versenken,
Dort ein ewig Bild zu malen:
Allvergessen, Eingedenken!

Träume, wie wenn Frühlingssonne
Aus dem Schnee die Blüten küsst,
Dass zu nie geahnter Wonne
Sie der neue Tag begrüsst,

Dass sie wachsen, dass sie blühen,
Träumend spenden ihren Duft,
Sanft an deiner Brust verglühen,
Und dann sinken in die Gruft.

Mathilde Wesendonk

DREAMS

Tell me, what wondrous dreams
hold my senses in thrall,
that they have not dissolved,
like empty bubbles, into nothingness?

Dreams that with every hour,
every day, bloom more sweetly,
and with their heavenly tidings
blissfully course through my heart?

Dreams that like a sublime radiance
penetrate the soul, there to paint
an everlasting image:
oblivion, remembrance!

Dreams, as when the Spring sun
kisses the blossoms out of the snow,
so that the new day welcomes them
to unsuspected bliss,

and they grow and bloom
and, dreaming, pour out their fragrance,
gently fade away upon your breast
and then sink into the tomb.

Mathilde Wesendonk
translation by Lionel Salter

Der Engel 1
Stehe still 9
Im Treibhaus 25
Schmerzen 34
Träume 41

WESENDONCK-LIEDER
(Mathilde Wesendonck)

Der Engel

Orch. Felix Mottl

Richard Wagner
1813-1883

EE 6696

Ernst Eulenburg Ltd

(sehr weich)
Fl.
Ob.
(sehr zart)
dim.
Cl. (B♭)
dim.
Fg.
Cor. (F)
(sehr zart)
dim.
Voce
- - - geln sa - gen, die des Him - mels heh - re Won - ne tau - schen mit der Er - den -
Vl. Solo
(senza sord.)
(zart)
ausdrucksvoll
Vl.
poco
Vle.
Vc.
Cb.
pizz.
arco
Pf.

13
Fl.
Ob.
I
p getragen
Cl. (B♭)
p getragen
p
Fg.
p getragen
p
Cor. (F)
II
pp
p
Voce
son-ne, dass, wo bang ein Herz in Sor - gen schmach-tet vor der Welt ver - bor - gen, dass, wo still es will ver-blu -
Vl. Solo
dim.
I
Vl.
dim.
II
dim.
I
Vle.
pp
II
dim.
I
Vc.
p
dim.
1. Solo
(senza sord.)
II
Pf.
p
p

18
Fl.
Ob.
Cl. (B♭)
Fg.
Cor. (F)
Voce
Vc.
Pf.
getragen
I
poco
(gesteigert, aber zart)
ten, und ver-gehn in Tränen - flu - ten, dass, wo brün - stig sein Ge - bet ein - zig um Er - lö - sung
1. Solo

23 poco rit.
a tempo
Fl.
Ob.
Cl. (B♭)
Fg.
Cor. (F)
Voce
Vl. Solo
Vl.
Vle.
Vc.
Cb.
Pf.
fleht, da der En - gel nie - - - - - - - - der schwebt, und es sanft gen Him-mel
(sul D)
immer p
dim.
più p
(sehr zart)
II (sehr zart)
(zart)
Tutti arco
pp
ppp
p

28
Fl.
Ob.
Cl. (B♭)
Fg.
Cor. (F)
Voce
Vl. I
Vl. II
Vle. I
Vle. II
Vc. Solo
Vc. I
Vc. II
Cb.
Pf.
p
pp
p poco cresc.
pp poco cresc.
(sehr ruhig)
hebt. Ja, es stieg auch mir ein En - - gel nie- der, und auf leuch - ten dem Ge-
poco cresc.
pp (sehr ruhig)
(col tutti Vc. I)
con sord.
dim.
pizz.
arco

34
Fl.
Ob.
Cl. (B♭)
Cor. (F)
Voce
Vl.
Vle.
Vc.
Cb.
Pf.
più cresc.
dim.
più p
a2
p dim.
I
mf
(mit Enthusiasmus)
(sanft)
-fie - der führt er fer - ne je-dem Schmerz, mei-nen Geist nun him - mel-
pp
pizz.
p

40
poco rit.
Fl.
Ob.
Cl.
(B♭)
Fg.
Cor.
(F)
Voce
- wärts!
Vl. Solo
Vl.
Vle.
Vc.
Cb.
Pf.
p cresc.
dim.
pp
ppp
più p

Stehe still

Orch. Felix Mottl

5
Cl. (B♭)
Fg.
I II
Cor. (F)
III IV
Voce
Mes - ser du der E - wig- keit; leuch - ten - de Sphä - ren im wei - ten All,
I
Vl.
II
arco
pizz.
Vle.
Vc.
arco
div.
pizz.
Cb.
arco
Pf.
cresc.

9
Cl.
(B♭)
Fg.
Cor.
(F)
I
II
III
IV
Voce
die ihr um-ringt den Wel - ten-ball; ur - e - wi-ge Schöp - fung, hal - te doch
Vl.
I
II
Vle.
Vc.
Cb.
Pf.
f
p
cresc.
arco
pizz.

13
Fl.
Ob.
Cl. (B♭)
Fg.
Cor. (F)
Tr. (C)
Voce
ein, ge-nug des Wer - dens, lass mich sein!
Vl.
Vla.
Vc.
Cb.
Pf.
a2
cresc.
f cresc.
pizz.

18
a2
Cl.
(B♭)
Fg.
I
II
Cor.
(F)
III
IV
Voce
Hal - te an dich, zeu - gen - de Kraft, Ur - ge - dan - ke, der e - wig schafft!
I
Vl.
II
pizz.
Vla.
Vc.
Pf.

22
Cl. (B♭)
Fg.
Cor. (F) I II
Voce
Vl. I II
Vla.
Vc.
Cb.
Pf.
arco
pizz.
p
cresc.
f
dim.
mf
Hem - met den A - tem, stil - let den Drang, schwei - get nur ei - ne Se - kun - de lang!

26
Fl.
Ob.
Cl. (B♭)
Fg.
Cor. (F)
Voce
Vl.
Vla.
Vc.
Cb.
Pf.
a2
cresc.
div.
Schwel - len-de Pul - se, fes - selt den Schlag; en - de, des Wol - lens ew' - ger

30
Fl.
Ob.
Cl. (B♭)
Fg.
Cor. (F)
Voce
Vl.
Vla.
Vc.
Cb.
Pf.
ff
ff dim.
a2
I
p
ausdrucksvoll
mf
f dim.
pp
p zart
Tag!
dass in se - lig süs - sem Ver - ges - -
div.
unis.
p getragen
f
p
arco
dim.

35
Ob.
dim.
Fg.
Cor. (F)
I II
I
pp
p (sehr weich)
III IV
p
Voce
-sen ich mög' al-le Won-nen er-mes - sen! Wenn Aug' in
Vl.
I
II
dim.
pp
p getragen
Vla.
Vc.
1. Solo
p sehr zart
Cb.
1. Solo
sul E
(ausdrucksvoll)
Pf.
p

42
Ob.
Cl. (B♭)
Fg.
Cor. (F)
I II
III IV
p getragen
p zart
pp
Voce
Au - ge won - nig trin - ken, See - - - le ganz
Vl.
Vla.
Vc.
(1. Solo)
Cb.
Pf.

49
Mässiger als zuvor
Ob.
Cl.
(B♭)
Fg.
Voce
in See - - le ver-sin - ken;
We - sen in We - sen sich
con sord.
pp
I
Vl.
II
con sord.
pp
Vla.
con sord.
pp
Solo
Vc.
Gli altri
pizz.
p
Solo
Cb.
Gli altri
pizz.
pp
con sord.
pp
Pf.
più p
pp

56
Fl.
Cl. (B♭)
Fg.
Cor. (F)
Tr. (C)
Voce
wie - der fin - det, und al - les Hof - fens En - de sich kün - det; die Lip - -
Vl.
Vla.
Solo
Vc.
Gli altri
Cb.
Pf.
più p
a2
pp
ppp
div.
pizz.
arco
(la metà)
(herabgestimmt)

63
Fl.
a2
pp
I
dim.
pp
Cl. (B♭)
Fg.
pp
pp
Cor. (F)
I II
III IV
pp
dim.
pp
dim.
Voce
-pe ver-stummt in stau - - nen - dem Schwei - - gen, kein-en
Vl.
I
II
pizz.
pp
Vla.
Solo
Vc.
Gli altri
con sord.
pp
ppp
Cb.
Pf.
EE 6696

70
Langsam
Fl.
Ob.
Cl. (B♭)
Fg.
Voce
(wie gänzlich) (sich verlierend)
Wunsch mehr will das Inn' - re zeu - gen: er - kennt der Mensch des
Vl.
arco
Vla.
Vc.
Tutti
Cb.
Pf.
(mit allmähliger

78
Fl.
Ob.
Cl. (B♭)
Fg.
Cor. (F)
Tr. (C)
Timp.
Voce
Vl.
Vla.
Vc.
Cb.
Pf.
poco a poco cresc.
senza sord.
cresc.
Ew' - gen Spur, und lös't dein Rät - sel, heil' - ge Na - tur!
Steigerung der Stärke)

87
Fl.
Ob.
Cl. (B♭)
Fg.
Cor. (F)
Tr. (C)
Timp.
Voce
Vl.
Vla.
Vc.
Cb.
Pf.
dim.
p
più p
pp
ppp

Im Treibhaus

Studie zu Tristan und Isolde
(Study for Tristan and Isolde)

Orch. Felix Mottl

6
Cl. (B♭)
Voce
Blät - ter-kro - nen, Bal-da-chi - ne von Sma - ragd, Kin - der ihr aus fer - nen Zo - nen, sa - get
Vl.
I
II
più p
pp
senza sord.
p ausdrucksvoll
Sola
Vle.
Gli altri
I
Vc.
II
Cb.
Pf.
p (ausdrucksvoll)

11
Fl.
Cl. (B♭)
Voce
mir wa-rum ihr klagt?
Schwei-gend nei-get ihr die Zwei-ge, ma-let Zei-chen in die
I
Vl.
II
con sord.
Sola
Vle.
Tutti
Gli altri
I
Vc.
II
Cb.
Pf.
più p

16
Fl.
I
p ausdrucksvoll
pp
Ob.
pp
Cl. (B♭)
I
pp
Fg.
pp
Voce
p
Luft, und der Lei - den stum - mer Zeu - ge, stei - get auf - wärts süs - ser Duft. Weit in
Vl.
I
II
pp
p
Vla.
pp
p
Vc.
p
Cb.
Pf.
pp
p
(ausdrucksvoll)
pp
p

22
Fg.
Voce
seh-nendem Ver-lan - gen brei-tet ihr die Ar - me aus, und um-schlin - get
Vl.
I
II
Vla.
Vc.
Cb.
Pf.
cresc.
dim.
27
poco rall.
wahn - be-fan - gen ö - de Lee -re nicht'-gen Graus. Wohl ich weiss es, ar - me Pflan-ze; ein Ge-
più p
div.
pp

33
Ob.
Fg.
Cor. (F)
Voce
-schi - cke tei - len wir, ob um - strahlt von Licht und Glan - ze, uns-re Heim - at ist nicht
Vl.
Vla.
Vc.
Cb.
Pf.
cresc.
dim.
molto
38
II (schwer)
hier! Und wie froh die Son - ne schei - det von des Ta - ges lee - rem Schein, hül-let
più p

43
Ob.
Cl.
(B♭)
Fg.
Cor.
(F)
Voce
Vl.
Vla.
Vc.
Cb.
Pf.
I
II
I. II.
I +
pp
p
dim.
der, der wahr - haft lei - det, sich in Schwei - gens Dun - kel ein. Stil - le wird's,
sul pont.

49
Cor. (F)
Voce
ein säu - selnd We - ben
fül - let bang den dun - klen
sul pont.
Vl.
Vla.
Cb.
più p
dim.
ppp
trem.
Pf.
54
Cl. (B♭)
Fg.
pp
poco p
più p
dim.
Raum:
schwe - re Trop-fen seh' ich schwe-ben an der Blät ter grü-nem Saum.
pizz.
senza sord.
Sola Vle.
Gli altri
poco

60
Fl.
Ob.
Cl. (B♭)
Fg.
Cor. (F)
Voce
Vl.
I
II
Vla.
Vc. (div.)
Cb.
Pf.
ppp
arco
pp
più p
div.
Tutti
pizz.
Tutti con sord.

Schmerzen

Orch. Felix Mottl

6
Ob.
p
Cl. (B♭)
p
Fg.
p
Cor. (F) I II
II
p
Tr. (C)
Voce
rot, wenn im Mee - res-spie - gel ba-dend dich er -reicht der frü-he Tod; doch er - steh'st in al - ter Pracht, Glo -
Vl. I
getragen
p
II
getragen
p
Vla.
getragen
p
Vc.
getragen
p
Cb.
getragen
p
Pf.
p
cresc.

10
Fl.
Ob.
Cl. (B♭)
Fg.
Cor (F)
Tr. (C)
Voce
Vl.
Vla.
Vc.
Cb.
Pf.
ausdrucksvoll
-ri-e der düstren Welt, du am Mor-gen neu er-wacht, wie ein-stol zer Sie - ges - held! Ach, wie

15
ausdrucksvoll
Fl.
mf dolce
Ob.
p dolce
Cl. (B♭)
Fg.
Cor. (F)
zart
dolce
dolce
Voce
soll - te ich da kla - gen, wie, mein Herz, so schwer dich sehn, muss die Son - ne selbst ver - za - gen, muss die
Vl.
Vla.
p
Vc.
p
Cb.
Pf.
dolce

18
poco rall.
Fl.
Ob.
ausdrucksvoll
a2
Cl. (B♭)
p cresc.
Fg.
cresc.
Cor. (F)
mit grosser Steigerung
Voce
Son-ne unter gehn? Und gebie - ret Tod nur Le-ben, geben Schmer - zen Won - ner
Vl.
cresc.
Vla.
Vc.
Cb.
Pf.

molto rit. a tempo
22
Fl.
Ob.
Cl. (B♭)
Fg.
Cor. (F)
Voce
nur: O wie dank' ich, dass gege-ben sol-che Schmer-zen mir Na - tur!
Vl.
Vla.
Vc.
Cb.
Pf.
dim.
cresc.

rit.
a tempo
27
Fl.
Ob.
Cl. (B♭)
Fg.
Cor. (F)
Tr. (C)
Vl.
Vla.
Vc.
Cb.
Pf.
verklingen
dim.
cresc.

Träume

Studie zu Tristan und Isolde
(Study for Tristan and Isolde)

Orch. Richard Wagner

* In the version for solo Violin and orchestra only
In der Fassung nur für Solovioline und Orchester

9
Cl.
(B♭)
poco cresc.
II
pp
Fg.
poco cresc.
dim.
più p
pp
Cor.
(F)
poco cresc.
dim.
più p
pp
Voce
Vl.S.
[sim.]
I
Vl.
[sim.]
II
dim.
più p
[sim.]
Vla.
dim.
più p
Vc.
dim.
più p
Pf.
dim.

16
II
Cl. (B♭)
Fg.
Cor. (F)
Voce
Sag', welch wunderba - re Träu - me hal - ten meinen Sinn um-
Vl.S.
I
Vl.
II
Vla.
Vc.
Pf.

23
II
Cl.
(B♭)
pp
pp
Fg.
pp
pp
Cor.
(F)
pp
pp
Voce
-fan - - gen, dass sie nicht wie lee - re Schäu - me sind in ö-des Nichts ver-
Vl.S.
p
più p
I
Vl.
II
pp
pp
Vla.
pp
Vc.
pp
Pf.

30
Cl. (B♭)
Fg.
Cor. (F)
Voce
gan - gen? Träu - - me, die in je-der Stun-de, je-dem Ta - ge schön - er blüh'n, und mit ih - rer
Vl.S.
Vl. I
Vl. II
Vla.
Vc.
Pf.
poco cresc.

36
Cl. (B♭)
Fg.
Cor. (F)
Voce
Vl.S.
Vl.
I
II
Vla.
Vc.
Pf.
pp
p
(belebt)
Him-mels-kun - de se - lig durch's Ge-mü - te ziehn? Träu - me, die wie
mf
dim.
più p
Ped.

42
rit.
Cl. (B♭)
Fg.
Cor. (F)
Voce
(steigernd)
heh-re Strahlen in die See - le sich ver-sen-ken, dort ein e-wig Bild zu ma - len: All - ver-ges - sen, Ein-ge-den - ken!
Vl.S.
Vl. I
Vl. II
Vla.
Vc..
Pf.

a tempo
48
Cl. (B♭)
Fg.
Cor. (F)
Voce
Vl.S.
I
Vl.
II
Vla.
Vc.
Pf.
f
dim.
p dolce
p (bewegt)
cresc.
dim.
Träu - - me, wie wenn Frühlings-sonne aus dem Schnee die Blü - ten küsst, dass zu nie ge - ahn-ter Won-ne sie der

54
Cl. (B♭)
Fg.
Cor. (F)
Voce
Vl.S.
Vl. I
Vl. II
Vla.
Vc.
Pf.
dim.
p dolce
più p
pp
(nachlassend)
(immer mehr nachlassend)
neu - e Tag be - grüsst, dass sie wach - sen, dass sie blü - hen, träu - mend spen - den ih - ren
dolce
p (weich)

60
Cl.
(B♭)
Fg.
Cor.
(F)
Voce
Duft, sanft an dei - ner Brust ver - glü - hen, und dann sin - ken
Vl.S.
più pp
più p
I
Vl.
II
Vla.
Vc.
pp
più p
Pf.
più p
morendo

67
Cl.
(B♭)
pp
Fg.
pp
Cor.
(F)
pp
Voce
in die Gruft.
Vl.S.
pp
I
Vl.
II
pp
Vla.
pp
Vc.
pp
Pf.
pp

*These notes are omitted in the version for solo violin